THE ENVISIONED DAWN

"NOT ALL MEN ARE SAME, SOME MOTHERS CLAIM THEM WITH FAME"

AJAY KUMAR SHAW

Contents

Contents

About Author

Ajay Kumar Shaw is working in a Government Organization under Ministry Of Defense. He comes from a modest society and medium financial background, so he is always grounded to earth. Being a science graduate (Physics) from Calcutta University he is gradually tending towards literature. Being in a hectic schedule he spends some time on his craze for writing. He lives in a world with unconventional things and his fantasies. He is aspiring for greater things from life apart from his current job. He likes reading love novels, writing stories, blogging, singing, dancing, interacting with different people and learning their language.

He believes **a person can't be a reader without being a writer and vice versa**. He keeps himself in trend among readers by reading the latest books published in the market. He has already participated in a few anthologies as a co-author and co-edited some books but this is his first solo book. Apart from this, he is scribbling for two romance novels which are expected to be published soon.

You can get to know about him and his books on:

IG: @soyajax

Blogs: https://innervoice97.wordpress.com/author/soyajax/

http://www.miraquill.com/soyajax

or you may reach out to him at ajayshaw545@gmail.com.

Author's Note

Hi readers,

First of all, I would like to thank y'all for choosing my book and spending your precious time on it. I hope that y'all will be able to relate to my perception of life and visualize my journey till here through these words.

It all started during initial lockdown days in March 2020. While people adopted new hobbies daily for vlogging during those quarantine days, I nurtured my hobby of writing. It was only then I had discovered my writing skills, however naive it may be. Professional writing was never my piece of cake but at the age of 22, it somehow just began.

My author friend Mr Ajay K Pandey used to say - 'write like a husband not like a writer', from which I made a lifetime note - anything I write, I'll always maintain my grassroot level. So all the poems which you will find inside depict my inner side with hardly any modifications.

It contains my vision or better to say my concept of modern independent women, some philosophical articles and some ironical write-ups regarding life. While some articles will definitely bring out the love dwelling in my heart since long time.

Hope this book will take you to a short emotional ride, portraying an obscure side of me.

- Ajay

1. WITH YOU TILL ETERNITY

I wanna make a place in you,
To recreate myself as new.
Be a Christian, Jedi or a Jew,
For me, what matter is just you.
Mine is fifty, yours are fifty.
Together we would break the nifty
Be at any stage, thirty or fifty
Would grow old with immense affinity.
Neither feminist, nor chauvinist,
Till the last day I would be a humanist.
Just like a leaf covered by the mist,
Our life would always co-exist.

2. CAUSE IT'S YOU

Plane gives me thrilling pain.
Journey's incomplete on a crowdy train.
It's due to sea, I have all gain
But, being with you on a shady lane,
Drives me crazy and insane.
On bare feet I'll walk of course,
On a never ending track, if you endorse.
No matter if hurdles comes with a lot of source,
You will be there, till the end of force.

3. SOMEDAY

The sky would be ideal pink,
Emotions attach with lifelong link,
Heart beats struggles with fierce blood,
Eyes almost full of teary flood,
Either is a skating rink.
Or near your kitchen sink.
You would see your eternal mate
Don't be late, instantly close your heart's gate,
And leave her not, be in any state.
That day you'll be in heaven's place,
Ending your life long weary chase.
I know it's hard to be practical
But the heart takes it as magical.

4. LIFE IT IS....

Simple ones are troubled a lot
Take my words, rest would have a chill pill shot.
People know how to utilize them well
At the time to felicitation, why they fail?
People say yes sir, yes ma'am
But I don't really give a damn.
Favors' give unworthy a pace,
Worthy ones are out of race.
What a fuckin shame!
Taking credit on others pain.
Dedication has a reverse impact
It's too late when you realize that.
Biasing is the motto of this game
People take proud on fake fame.
My nature makes me as I am ,
I always keep burning my own lamp.

5. SHE'S MOM, AFTERALL

There's no place like mother's lap.
Neither in any app, nor on a diverse map.
Even in her shout, scold and slap,
There is guidance for future's mishap
Never take her for granted,
Because you are getting things, before you wanted.
Guess, how much she was dedicated?
That you have been perfectly malted.
Ask the ones, who are deprived of these,
Are eating curry without the cheese.
It's not a thing to be taken at lease
Mothers serve that all without fees.
She bears the enormous pain to take you out.
With plenty of groan, moan and shout.
If you think yourself worthy of being out,
Make her always laugh out loud.

6. HERO BY FACE , HOLLOW FROM BASE….

Maturity level is at it's peak .
Folks are going mentally sick,
Making our youth power gradually weak.
China has found out a fuck'in technique.
Hello, like, bigo, Vigo and ticktok,
How shitty is this stock!
Making us does lip-sync and mock,
Fading our senses as a stumbling block.
Majority of contents flowing around,
Showing immortal things with a big sound
Taking fake fame on a creativity ground,
Pretending to be a damn artist renowned.
This mania is spreading like a flue,
Obsessed by people like creepy glue.
Make them flourish in a curious or a zoo
My only gratitude to them is ahh thhuuu!

7. LIBRA

When there is a will, there is a way,
He is the perfect one to obey.
He can find silver lining to every cloud,
Search his past, he was always wowed.
His charm can't be denied upon,
Once got influenced, you can't move on.
His love is not a onetime fling
Unless you're done, he can perform a lifelong cling.
Hard work is a part of him,
Which makes him well deserved from cream.

8. RELATIONS – THE MOST FRAGILE TING

Relations fade in a lifelong chase,
It burns on the fuel of praise.
Just like a seedling in a vase,
It requires care, patience and little embrace.
Sometimes money is the only thing
Especially when it comes about your rings.
Make her dance, make her sing,
Wish each other a very happy ageing.
Relations are like a chemical linkage.
Completing each other with ion exchange.
It grows old with permanent bondage,
Provide, there is a mutual engage.

9. THOSE DAYS

Those were the golden days,
When minds were in unbiased phase,
Had a craze on TV and lays,
And were aloof from any daze.
When dreams changed with every frame,
We were too much sensible of our name
When classmates cry out puppy shame
We used to play a cute blame.
When mom's spank was the cruelest thing,
Still her lap made me pretend as king,
From serious aching to silly actions,
Dad took care of each and everything.

10. NOT YOUR CUP OF TEA

I may be awkward some time
Is this a serious crime?
But when I am in my prime,
You would require me all the time.
You call me introvert, I don't care ,
In me assessment , I am fair .
My feelings are for few, others I don't share ,
Cause they are selected, whom I care.
My methods are unconventional.
They start afresh from a new angle.
That's the reason , in actual
You always find me in futile quarrel.

11. SOLDIER WRITES......

We too have sort of craze,
Still we're not on a same page.
We're bound to an apparent cage,
While there's no restriction on your outage.
Nine to five is what you do.
Dare someday to be a part of crew.
Many of you don't even have a clue,
What we actually go through.
In bad times, you're not alone
For good news, we only have cell phone.
Sometimes night are full of groan,
While you take pleasure in fussy moan.

12. TI'S YOU AND ME

Gazing the starts throughout the night,
It's you and me.
Road side tea with tea and marine lite,
It's you and me.
Singing our heart loud, being very tight,
It's you and me.
Getting drenched on a rainy night,
It's you and me.
Hugs and kisses after casual fights,
It's you and me.
Assisting me in flying kite,
It's you and me.
Sharing every sip and bite,
It's you and me.
On a long walk under din streetlight,
It's you and me.
These are all, if you plight
To be always with me.

13. SOULMATE

Who-so —ever she is
I wonder how lucky she is!
For me and her as well.
Coming along in a lifelong spell
Taking care of each other's desire
Setting our hearts on fervid fire
Stepping into a world, knit so well
No less than a fairy tale.
They call it bullshit and futile
Nothing matters except her smile
From white-grey matter to tabular vein
Love anaesthetizes every pain.

14. A REUNION TO MAKE

A brassbound reunion to make,
A dream since long, for old time's sake,
Recreating old memories not for fake
With music, champagne and cake.
Of all mates of my schooling days,
A day to be spared for daily chase
To relive our golden phase,
A day full of appreciation and praise.
Trying ten years challenge for real,
Keeping aloof all social media deal
To express everyone , what I feel?
Longing for you all with a great zeal.

15. LOVE IS FRIENDSHIP

A girl and a boy can't remain friends for long
Here you can't judge right or wrong
Because zaika of love and friendship are pretty same
Trust understanding can change the game.
It starts with 'just friends' you know
But gradually mind can't draw line between the duo.
A friend can make a better match , in fact
Better than any matrimony, tinder or chit –chat.

16. DANCE YOUR HEART OUT

Dance is a feel which makes you live,
Be it salsa, tango or a jive.
Cause dance show the way you feel.
How intimate can you go with your zeal?
Dance gives you the reason to trust.
Your moves speak more than you have discussed.
Embrace her well, let her feel your intentions,
Her company would fade away all your tension.
Let her breath match your beat,
Ignite a spark for never ending heat.
Face-to-face, hand-to-hand, eye-to eye,
Dude, you will be seventh sky.

17. STORIES

What makes us living? – a story.
Fundamental unit of a human-a story,
A writer's opinion on existence of any sort of story.
Whatever the science says, but this is my theory.
What is our worth without a story?
Just like a country without its glory.
Each of us has something to share – a story
From dhabas to school's backyard, everywhere there's a story,
What people lack is a company for their story?
Swiping through the screen, will that make a sroey?
Making far ones close and close ones far away,
What an irony!
Bewitching ourselves like bees over honey.
Men are mortal, not their stories.
There's a limitation for your stories.
So live your moments to its extent and make stories,,
Cause we want a house not innumerable storey.
Moving fingers instead of legs and gazing
Screen instead of face, will that make a story?

18. IT'S YOU BABE…..

Her tangling hairs,
Like mushy feathers full of bouncy layers.
Her kissable lips, cruelly suppressed
Oh god! How much I m obsessed.
Her aroma of which I've gone mad about
The only cure to my volatile shout.
Her minutest thing is a priority to me
There's nothing in me, if not she.
Never found someone so ravishing in saree,
With mesmerizing spell of so called Indian Nari.
Her partially visible tattoo on the waist
and never ending eyeliner make me fully obsessed.

19. INDEPENDENCE?A LONG WAY TO GO…..

Yipee yippee! Yay yay?
It's our Independence day.
We're in seventy-fifth year of independence.
Yet following our trend of descendance.

20. SHE'S A GIRL

She's is a girl,
Worthy enough to be called as a pearl.
Not so mature, yet sensible.
I warn, don't underestimate her as a feeble.
She's my sister,
She's cool and can cause blister.
Her lifelong recognition is all I want,
Overcome all obstructions and remain like a shunt
Our relationship can't be recorded as a reel
But , I can always feel.
I don't need a knot to be taut,
For always keeping you in my thought.
I have many siblings till date,
But you are and will remain my favorite.

21. IT'S YOUR WEDDING NIGHT...

If she's sleeping, let her sleep
She vowed to be your wife, not your keep
Tell your in-laws not to investigate and peep
Be the chance, else every man is called creep.
Give her space, let her adjust
She barely knows you, how can she trust?
Your work won't be done with force and thrust,
Try to be her best friend first.
She would definitely respect your patience.
She's a girl man, sensible in her essence.
Your puerility will drive you in search of complacence
But only she can complete your valence.

22. ONCE A BESTFRIEND, ALWAYS A BESTFRIEND...............

As the best player can't be the captain of the team.
Likewise, your best friend can't be the man of your dream.
Although no one else deserves to be her man,
Your destiny seems to have some different plan.
Life partner is greater than the best friend, it's possible.
Life partner is less than a best friend, strongly possible.
Then why the hell can't both be the same?
This inequality makes me insane.
Best friend is always best
You may attach my suffix to the rest
Be it best partner, lover or husband,
In all forms, he will remain constant.